How to use the course

1 Look at the pictures with your child. Talk about the spread together in your own language, using the pictures to help you to figure out what the English means.

2 Read through the English again, this time listening to the recording.

3 Then read through the words on the pages together. Take turns to read the different parts.

4 Play the recording again, this time encouraging your child to repeat the words / phrases after Abby and Zak.

5 When your child is feeling confident, play some games to help him / her remember the language he / she has just learned:

- Ask what words mean (in English or your own language).

- See how many of the words your child can remember in English without looking at the book.

- Practice the words together in different contexts (e.g. practice numbers using toys or coins, colors using things around the house, family / clothes using photographs).

6 Encourage your child to move on to reading the book and listening to the recording independently.

Testing and

- **EAZ** contains [...] you and your child meas[...] progress. These come after every [...] spreads and test the language just learned. Each quiz has a reward activity (see pp.42–43).

- The book also has a Wordlist, featuring all the important words used in the course (see pp.46–47). Encourage your child to copy out some of the words and to write the meaning of the words in his / her own language. You can use this to test your child – or your child can use it to test himself / herself, by covering up one of the languages and trying to give the translation.

- Encourage your child to create his / her own illustrated wordlist. This will make the words much easier to remember.

- If your child is interested in finding out other words in English, buy a children's bilingual dictionary and look up words together.

Testing and reviewing are an important part of language learning, but they should be fun. Above all, don't forget to praise and reward your child's efforts.

Have fun learning English with Abby and Zak!

And friends!

3

American English

with **Abby** and **Zak**

Contents

Text by Tracy Traynor
Illustrations by Laura Hambleton

Milet

For parents and teachers

English with Abby and Zak

is specially for children aged 5–10.

Children can use it to start learning English or to improve their English. It introduces words and phrases in subjects that children meet every day – family, friends, school, activities, etc.

Children learn languages best if the learning is enjoyable. This is why **EAZ** is colorful and interactive, full of fun characters and challenging quizzes.

To get the most out of it

- Learn along with your child or encourage him / her to learn with a friend.
- Join in with the lively recordings.
- Make testing and reviewing as you go along competitive and fun.
- Use **EAZ** like a storybook, not a textbook.
- Remember to praise and reward your child's efforts.
- See the notes on p.3 for further suggestions on how to use the course.

Each spread (two-page section) in the book is on a new topic.
Here is a typical spread, with the most important features labeled.

I can say . . .
Checklist for learner to use at the end of spread

Look at this!
Summary of the language structures

Language to learn

Recording
Cue to listen to Abby and Zak on the recording and join in.

I can say . . .

Hello!

Bye!

My name's . . .

What's your name?

The alphabet

Let's count!

0 zero
1 one
2 two
3 three
4 four
5 five

I'm eight.

HAPPY BIRTHDAY

Look at this!

one balloon
ten balloons

I'm eight.
He's nine.
She's eight.

Match

My	you, Zak!
What's	old are you?
How	ten.
I'm	name's Abby.
See	your name?

Find and color

seven two zero six ten one eight four three nine five

Write

__Hi!__ My name's Abby.

What's your _____ ?

Hello! _____ name's Zak.

_____ eight.

_____ your name?

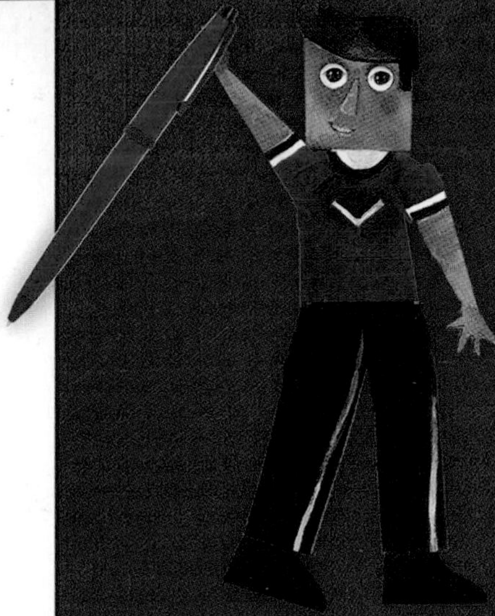

Count

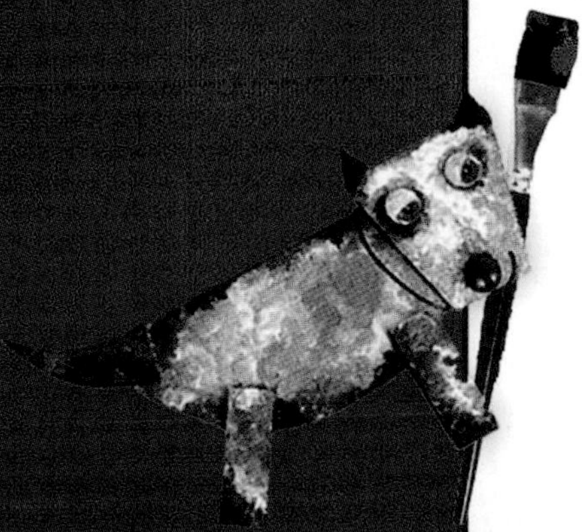

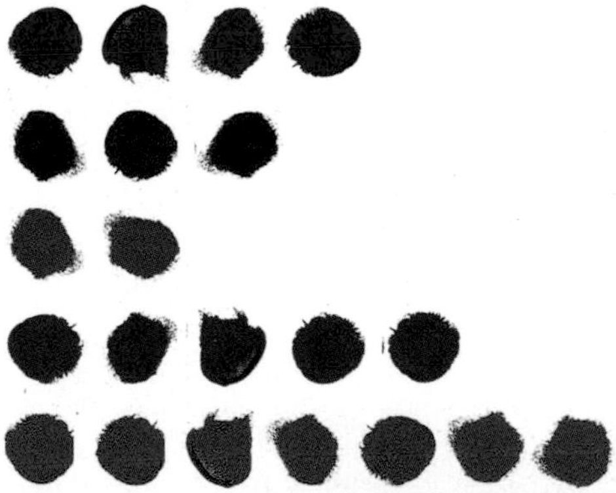

four
_____

_____

_____

_____

_____

Draw and write

My name's _____

I'm _____

Good job!
Go to p.42.

11

My family

my sister →

my brothers ↓

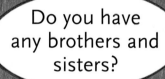

Do you have any brothers and sisters?

Look at this!

Do you have any brothers and sisters?

I **have** two brothers and one sister.

I **have no** sisters.

I can say . . .

This is my . . . ˇˇˇ

Do you have any brothers and sisters? ˇˇˇ

I have one brother and two sisters. ˇˇˇ

Say it with Abby and Zak! • Say it with Abby and Zak!

We live here!

This is my house.

my bedroom

my mom and dad's bedroom

the bathroom

the stairs

This is the garden.

I can say . . .

This is my house.

This is the hall.

Look at this!

This is **my** bedroom.

This is Ben**'s** bedroom.

Ben's bedroom

the living room

the hall

the kitchen

Say it with Abby and Zak!

This is my house.

Quiz 2

Find and color

brotherdadgrandmasistermomgrandpa

Write

head

Find and write

lalh _____ hall _____

chikten _____

bmoorhat _____

vingli moro _____

denrag _____

Match

Do you have any	living room.
This is	brother.
I have one	four o'clock.
This is the	my bedroom.
It's	brothers and sisters?

Draw and write

Good job!
Go to p.42.

This is my _____

21

The sun
is yellow.

The panda is
black and white.

The umbrella is
blue and purple.

I can say . . . .

I like blue.

I don't like green.

It's a red car.

The sun is yellow.

I like . . .

It's . . .

a red apple

a green car

a pink mug

an orange
flower

Look at this!

a car

an + a, e, i, o, u

an apple

Say it with Abby and Zak!

Say it with Abby and Zak!

23

At school

Quiz 3

Color

a red T-shirt

a yellow and green baseball cap

a pink sweater

a purple hat

an orange dress

blue pants

Write

I'm pants wearing   <u>I'm wearing pants.</u>

like purple I   _____

green I like don't   _____

The yellow sun is   _____

you are How ?   _____

Find and circle (10 things at school!)

p	i	c	t	u	r	e	b
a	b	c	h	a	i	r	o
i	n	g	r	e	e	a	o
n	e	p	o	d	e	s	k
t	q	l	i	c	n	e	p
s	c	i	s	s	o	r	s
c	r	a	y	o	n	s	t

Draw and write

I'm wearing _____

_____

_____

_____

Good job!
Go to p.43.

I'm a pirate!

I'm a fairy.

I'm a cowboy.

I'm a witch.

I'm a monster.

Look at this!

Are you a . . . ?

Yes, I am.

No, I'm not.

I can say . . .

I'm a pirate.

Are you a wizard?

Yes, I am.

No, I'm not.

Say it with Abby and Zak!
Say it with Abby and Zak!

I want to . . .

play hide and seek

bounce

read

Do you want to play?

Yes, I do.

play soccer

watch TV

I can say . . .

I want to bounce.

Do you want to play?

Yes, I do.

No, I don't.

Say it with Abby and Zak!

35

doll

duck

teddy
bear

scooter

I'm going to
buy a guitar.

dinosaur

guitar

I'm going to
buy a ball.

I can say . . .

a doll, a ball

I'm going to buy
a teddy bear.

Say it with Abby and Zak!

37

In the café

I can say . . .

I'd like pizza, please.

I'd like apple juice, please.

Thank you!

Look at this!

I'd like pizza, strawberries, and lemonade, please.

Quiz 4

Match

Yes,	a witch?
I want	I'm not.
Are you	I am.
No,	a rocking horse.
I'm going to buy	to bounce.

Write

Do you ___want___ to bounce?   read

Yes, I _____ .   ~~want~~

No, I _____ .   bike

I want to _____ .   swim

I want to ride my _____ .   do

I want to _____ a book.   don't

I'm going to buy a . . .

niatr _____train_____

rootsce _____

ritagu _____

dydte arbe _____

ckgniro seroh _____

Write

I'd like pasta and orange juice, please.

_____

_____

_____

Do you want to play?

Draw and write

Good job! Go to p.43.

I want to _____

_____

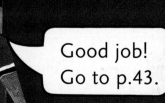
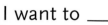

41

Quiz answers

Quiz 1

Find and color

seven, two, zero, six, ten, one
eight, four, three, nine, five

Match

My name's Abby.
What's your name?
How old are you?
I'm ten.
See you, Zak!

Count

four
three
two
five
seven

Write

Hi! My name's Abby.
What's your **name**?
Hello! **My** name's Zak.
I'm eight.
What's your name?

Quiz 2

Find and write

hall, kitchen, bathroom,
living room, garden

Find and color

brother, dad,
grandma,
sister, mom,
grandpa

Match

Do you have any
brothers and sisters?
This is my bedroom.
I have one brother.
This is the living room.
It's four o'clock.

Write

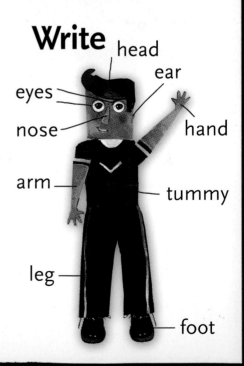

head
ear
eyes
nose
hand
arm
tummy
leg
foot

Find and color

- ● a red T-shirt
- ●● a yellow and green baseball cap
- ● a pink sweater
- ● blue pants
- ● an orange dress
- ● a purple hat

Quiz 3

Write

I'm wearing pants.
I like purple.
I don't like green.
The sun is yellow.
How are you?

Find and circle

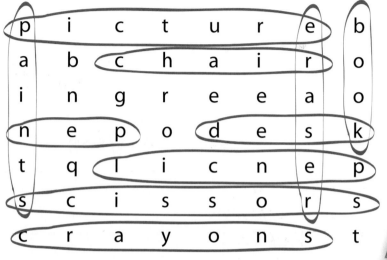

p	i	c	t	u	r	e	b
a	b	c	h	a	i	r	o
i	n	g	r	e	e	a	o
n	e	p	o	d	e	s	k
t	q	l	i	c	n	e	p
s	c	i	s	s	o	r	s
c	r	a	y	o	n	s	t

Match

Yes, I am.
I want to bounce.
Are you a witch?
No, I'm not.
I'm going to buy a rocking horse.

Write

Do you **want** to bounce?
Yes, I **do**.
No, I **don't**.
I want to **swim**.
I want to ride my **bike**.
I want to **read** a book.

Find and write

I'm going
to buy a . . .

book, **scooter**, **guitar**, **teddy bear**, **rocking horse**

Write

I'd like pasta and orange juice, please.
I'd like fish sticks and ice cream, please.
I'd like a burger and lemonade, please.
I'd like apple juice, a sandwich, and strawberries, please.

Quiz 4

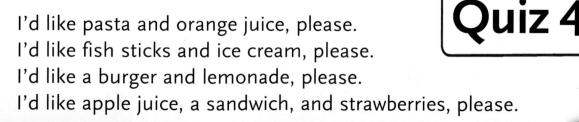

Wordlist

Aa
a/an
and
And you?
apple juice
Are you . . . ?
arm

Bb
ball
balloon
baseball cap
bathroom
bedroom
bedtime
best friend
black
blue
board
book
boots
bounce
breakfast time
brother
burger
Bye!

Cc
calculator
car

chair
cold
cool
cowboy
crayons
crocodile
cute

Dd
dad
dance
desk
dinnertime
dinosaur
Do you have
any . . . ?
Do you want
to . . . ?
doll
dollhouse
draw
dress
duck

Ee
ear
eight
elephant
eleven
eraser
eyes

Ff
fairy
fish sticks
five
flower
foot
four
french fries
friend

Gg
garden
giraffe
glasses
glue
Good job!
grandma
grandpa
grasshopper
green
guitar
gym shoes

Hh
hall
hand
hat
head
Hello!
Here you are.

He's . . .
Hi!
hippo
hot
house
How are you?
How do you feel?
hungry

Ii
I don't like . . .
I have . . .
I like . . .
I want to . . .
I'd like . . .
I'm . . .
I'm wearing . . .
ice cream
It's six o'clock.

Jj
jacket

Kk
kangaroo
kitchen

Ll
leg
lemonade

living room
lots of
lunchtime

Mm
magician
mom
monkey
monster
morning
mug
my
My name's . . .

Nn
nine
no
nose
notebook

Oo
one
orange
orange juice

Pp
paintbrush
paints
panda
pants

paper
pasta
pen
pencil
picture
pink
pirate
pizza
play soccer
play hide and seek
playtime
please
purple

Rr
race car
read
red
ride my bike
rocking horse
ruler

Ss
sandwich
school
school uniform
scissors
scooter
See you!
seven

She's . . .
shirt
shoes
shorts
silly
sister
six
skirt
smart
snake
skates
stairs
strawberries
student
sun
sunglasses
sweater
swim

Tt
talk to my friend
teacher
teddy bear
ten
thank you
the
There's . . .
There are . . .
thirsty
This is . . .

three
tie
toy
train
T-shirt
tummy
twelve
two

Uu
umbrella

Ww
watch TV
What's your name?
What time is it?
What would
you like?
white
window
witch
wizard

Yy
yellow
yes
You look . . .

Zz
zero

American English

with **Abby** and **Zak**

Milet Publishing
333 North Michigan Avenue
Suite 530
Chicago, IL 60601
info@milet.com
www.milet.com

English with Abby and Zak
Text by Tracy Traynor
Illustrations by Laura Hambleton

Adapted from British to American English by Eleise Jones

*Thanks to Livia and Abby for
all their good ideas. TT*

With special thanks to Scott. LH

First published by Milet Publishing, LLC in 2007

ISBN-13: 978 1 84059 4911
ISBN-10: 1 84059 491 8

Printed and bound in China

Please see our website www.milet.com
for other language learning books featuring Abby and Zak.